ISAAC
NEWTON

LEGENDS AND LEGACIES

THE BIOGRAPHY OF
ISAAC NEWTON

Published by
Rupa Publications India Pvt. Ltd 2024
7/16, Ansari Road, Daryaganj
New Delhi 110002

Sales centres:
Bengaluru Chennai
Hyderabad Jaipur Kathmandu
Kolkata Mumbai Prayagraj

Copyright © Rupa Publications India Pvt. Ltd 2024

The views and opinions expressed in this book are the authors' own and the facts are as reported by him which have been verified to the extent possible, and the publishers are not in any way liable for the same.

All rights reserved.
No part of this publication may be reproduced, transmitted, or stored in a retrieval system, in any form or by any means, electronic, mechanical, photocopying, recording or otherwise, without the prior permission of the publisher.

P-ISBN: 978-93-6156-175-7
E-ISBN: 978-93-6156-551-9

First impression 2024

10 9 8 7 6 5 4 3 2 1

Printed in India

This book is sold subject to the condition that it shall not, by way of trade or otherwise, be lent, resold, hired out, or otherwise circulated, without the publisher's prior consent, in any form of binding or cover other than that in which it is published.

Contents

Introduction	7
Early Life (1642-1661)	9
University Education and Early Work (1661-1665)	14
Newton's Year of Wonders (1665-1666)	20
Return to Cambridge and Academic Career	31
Later Career and Public Service (1696-1727)	58
Personal Life and Character	70
Recognition and Honors	76

Introduction

Many people believe that Isaac Newton is the single most important person in the history of the world. This is due to the fact that the Newtonian revolution had a significant impact on the development of world history. Because of this, many people believe that his ideas altered the course of history, and that things would have been quite different if he and his theory had not been developed. Because we do not know what would have happened "if things had been different," it is impossible to discuss claims like this in a precise manner. This is because we do not know what would have happened. Furthermore, neither Newton nor anyone else can emerge from nothing; what Newton did was built upon and partially created by the work of others, and it originated from general trends and beliefs that were prevalent in the world at that time.

In other words, Newton did not come from nothing. For the purpose of putting this into perspective, this kind of question has been a topic of discussion among historians (and writers like Tolstoy) for centuries. Considering it through the lens of a turbulent flow is one way to think about it. One more way is that, on occasion, at a crucial juncture in the progression of history, relatively

Sir Isaac Newton

minor disturbances can develop into significant repercussions, and a relatively small group of individuals can have a significant impact on the larger trajectory of history. The great whirlpools and eddies of history, on the other hand, control large movements and masses of people over extended periods of time, and there is not much that can be done to change them. With regard to the situation involving Isaac Newton, it is unmistakable that the time was right for a revolution in the scientific community. While Newton himself acknowledged that he was building on previous work, he also acknowledged that he was performing a synthesis of his own to some extent. He is credited with making the following famous remark: "If I have seen further than others, it is because I have been standing on the shoulders of giants." This remark was made to Robert Hooke, which is an interesting fact.

Nevertheless, a great deal is dependent on the particulars of the execution; the manner in which he formulated his dynamics was of the utmost importance.

Having a sufficient understanding of the significance of what he was doing and the significance of the significant break that it was going to make with the past, Newton was able to effectively carry out his actions. Consequently, in spite of the intimidating nature of the Principia, which is considered to be his masterwork, it was structured in such a way that it not only provided a definitive formulation of what was later referred to as classical dynamics, but it also presented a new and extremely significant philosophical perspective. For this reason, the Principia is considered to be his masterpiece. In the field of physics, when new fundamental theories are developed, they always reinterpret the world, and this is a quality that is shared by all of these theories.

1

Early Life (1642-1661)

Isaac Newton was born on December 25, 1642, in the rural manor house of Woolsthorpe, near Grantham in Lincolnshire. According to Newton, his early life was perilous due to his small and fragile size, being so tiny that he could fit inside a quart pot. His father, a yeoman farmer, had died three months before his birth. Though not wealthy, Newton's father left a substantial will. When Newton was three years old, his mother remarried Barnabas Smith, the rector of a neighboring village, and Newton was left in the care of his grandparents. Biographers suggest that this separation deeply affected Newton, contributing to his irritable and insecure adult personality. Little is known about Newton's early childhood except that he attended day schools in nearby villages. When Newton was ten, his mother returned to Woolsthorpe with three children from her second marriage after Barnabas Smith had passed away.

> **Fun Fact:** Newton was so uninterested in farming that he would bribe the servant to take his place at the market while he stayed home to read and experiment.

Education at Grantham

At the age of twelve, Newton was enrolled in a grammar school in Grantham. Here, he studied Latin, Greek, and the Bible, absorbing the canons of the Anglican Protestant Religion. Despite starting in the lowest class, he became the top student through sheer determination. Newton, described as a "sober, silent, thinking lad," preferred the company of girls and had little interaction with other boys. He had a documented adolescent romance with Miss Storer, the stepdaughter of Mr. Clark, an apothecary with whom Newton lived during his school years in Grantham. Newton's fascination with "strange inventions and mechanical works" during this time is well-documented. He created various models and designs, including kites, dolls' furniture, and a crank-operated four-wheeled vehicle. He also crafted numerous sundials and was an accomplished draughtsman.

> **Fun Fact:** Newton built a small windmill powered by a mouse running on a treadmill, showcasing his early inventive spirit.

Historical Context: England's Upheaval

Newton's formative years coincided with significant upheaval in England. In 1649, when Newton was seven, Charles I was executed, and Oliver Cromwell established Puritan rule. After Cromwell's death, Charles II restored the monarchy in 1660. Charles II's reign, from 1660 to 1685, was relatively peaceful despite a naval war with the Protestant Dutch, secretly subsidized by the French under the "Treaty of Dover." However, constitutional issues remained unresolved, and a fictional 'Popish plot' in 1678 led to the exclusion of Catholics from Parliament and key positions. Charles II's later attempts to increase royal prerogative ultimately failed.

> **Fun Fact:** Newton was born in the same year Galileo Galilei died, marking a symbolic passing of the scientific torch.

Galileo Galilei

Influences of the English Civil War on His Early Life

Newton's early years were deeply influenced by the political turmoil of the English Civil War. Born in 1642, the year the Civil War began, he grew up amidst the conflict between the Royalists, who supported King Charles I, and the Parliamentarians, led by Oliver Cromwell. This war resulted in the execution of Charles I in 1649, when Newton was seven years old, and the establishment of the Commonwealth under Cromwell's Puritanical rule.

Newton's family, being yeoman farmers, were likely affected by the economic and social disruptions caused by the war. The war's impact on the rural economy may have contributed to the financial constraints his family faced. Additionally, the political and religious upheavals during this period may have shaped Newton's intellectual development, fostering a sense of independence and resilience.

After Cromwell's death in 1658, the monarchy was restored in 1660 with Charles II's return to the throne. This period, known as the Restoration, brought relative peace but did not resolve underlying constitutional issues. Newton's formative years coincided with these significant events, which influenced the social and educational environment in which he grew up.

Oliver Cromwell

King Charles II

Although the English Civil War had ended before Newton's birth, its repercussions influenced his early life. The conflict had devastated England, affecting social and economic conditions. Newton's family experienced the war's aftermath, which shaped his upbringing and future endeavors. The war's influence on education and scientific inquiry in England indirectly impacted Newton, contributing to the intellectual environment he grew up in.

The years 1665-1666 at Woolsthorpe were a period of remarkable creativity and productivity for Isaac Newton. During this time, he made groundbreaking advances in mathematics, mechanics, and optics, laying the foundations for his later work. His formulation of calculus, exploration of the nature of light, and insights into the laws of motion and gravity emerged from this period of intense intellectual activity. The annus mirabilis solidified Newton's reputation as one of the greatest scientific minds in history.

2

University Education and Early Work (1661-1665)

College Life at Cambridge

Upon arrival at Cambridge, Newton enrolled at Trinity College, reflecting the upper-class mores of English society. At Trinity, he started as a subsizar, performing menial tasks to earn his keep, as his mother was unwilling to fund further education. Despite Cambridge's Aristotelian curriculum, Newton began exploring

Trinity College

UNIVERSITY EDUCATION AND EARLY WORK (1661-1665)

various philosophical and scientific works, recording his thoughts in a notebook titled "Quaestiones Quaedam Philosophicae." He delved into the works of Galileo, Hobbes, More, Boyle, Plato, Aristotle, and particularly Descartes, whose ideas greatly intrigued him. Newton's experiments with light and vision during this period were extensive, sometimes risking his sight.

> **Fun Fact:** Newton once stared at the sun until he saw spots to study the effects of light on his vision.

René Descartes   **Plato**   **Aristotle**   **Boyle**

Early Years at Cambridge

During the period of time between 1666 and 1689, Newton spent the majority of his time working at Cambridge University. His first obstacle was the election for a fellowship, which he had to deal with right from the start of his journey. In the event that he were to emerge victorious, he would be able to maintain his current employment and would also be able to obtain a permanent position at the college.

At the College of the "Holy and Undivided Trinity" on October 2, 1667, Newton was given the position of fellow during that year. When Newton arrived, it was for the very first time. As part of his commitment, he stated that he would "embrace the true religion of Christ with all my soul." Additionally, he agreed to fulfil the obligation to "take holy orders when the time prescribed by these statutes arrives, or resign from the college." It was pretty much the only thing that was expected of a man by society. Without a doubt, the most important thing was to steer clear of "the three sins of crime, heresy, and marriage." This happened to be the most significant thing. Given the circumstances, it would appear that Newton was extremely busy during this time period. In addition to carrying on with his work in optics, he also developed an interest in alchemy, which he would go on to study for at least thirty years more after that. Furthermore, throughout the course of his life, he became even more isolated than he had been before. However, during this time period, he was engaged in a significant interaction with the outside world. This interaction took place during this time period.

Influence of Isaac Barrow

During the beginning of the year 1669, Newton was given a new book that had been written by Nicholas Mercator. The book was given to Newton by Isaac Barrow, who was the first Lucasian professor of mathematics at Cambridge's Cambridge University. In order to calculate the sum of a series for the expression log(1+x), Barrow had obtained it from the mathematician Collins, and Mercator had utilised it in order to calculate the sum of the series. Newton immediately became aware of the fact that other mathematicians

Isaac Barrow

UNIVERSITY EDUCATION AND EARLY WORK (1661-1665)

would soon discover the very general results for series that he had discovered in Woolsthorpe, despite the fact that he had discovered them first. This was despite the fact that Newton had discovered them first. After that, he handed over a piece of writing that he had penned.

LOGARITHMO-TECHNIA:
SIVE
Methodus construendi
LOGARITHMOS
Nova, accurata, & facilis;
SCRIPTO
Antehàc Communicata, Anno Sc. 1667.
Nonis *Augusti* : Cui nunc accedit
Vera Quadratura Hyperbolæ,
&
Inventio *Summæ* Logarithmorum.

AUCTORE *NICOLAO MERCATORE*
Holsato, è Societate Regia.

HUIC ETIAM JUNGITUR
MICHAELIS ANGELI RICCII Exercitatio
Geometrica de Maximis & Minimis; hìc ob Argumenti
præstantiam & Exemplarium raritatem recusa.

LONDINI,
Typis *Guilielmi Godbid*, & Impensis *Mosis Pitt* Bibliopolæ, in vico vulgò vocato *Little Britain*. Anno M. DC. LXVIII.

Nicolaus Mercator Logarithmotechnia

The title of the paper was "De Analysi per aequationes numeroinfinitorum infinitas," which translates to "On the analysis of infinite series" in English. The paper detailed the most significant discoveries that he had made. Considering that Newton was naturally reserved and wanted to avoid being observed by the general public at this particular juncture, Barrow had to exert a great deal of pressure on Newton to send this. This was necessary because Newton wanted to avoid being observed by the general public. Collins disseminated copies of the manuscript to a number of different individuals, despite the fact that he was not permitted to reveal the manuscript to anyone. In this very moment, the young Newton was presented with the opportunity to meet mathematicians from other locations besides Cambridge for the very first time.

COMMERCIUM
EPISTOLICUM
D. JOHANNIS COLLINS,
ET ALIORUM
DE
ANALYSI
PROMOTA:
JUSSU
SOCIETATIS REGIÆ
In lucem editum.

LONDINI:
Typis Pearsonianis, Anno M DCC XII.

Ex Bibl.
Ios. Ren. C...
Imperialis.

John Collins Commercium Epistolicum

Not long after that, in October of 1669, Newton was appointed to the position of Lucasian professor of mathematics, making him the second Lucasian professor of mathematics in the history of the field. In recognition of Barrington's efforts, Newton was presented with the opportunity to be promoted to one of the eight endowed professorships that are available at the university. So that he could fulfil his role as chaplain to the king, he decided to step down from his position as a professor. This allowed him to accomplish his goal. Considering everything that had transpired, it was challenging for Newton to cut himself off from the rest of the world entirely. His requests for assistance from Newton were persistent, and at one point, Collins even held an early draft of Newton's theory of fluxions in his hands. Collins was persistent in his requests for assistance from Newton. On the other hand, Newton made a request for it to be returned, and Collins never saw it again after that.

Discovery of Mathematics

Newton discovered his passion for mathematics around 1663, a subject barely taught at school or university. By 1664, he had begun acquiring advanced books on geometry, algebra, and infinite series. His solitary study allowed him to absorb a significant amount of contemporary mathematics, fostering his interest in both its pure form and practical applications. However, to continue his studies, Newton needed a college scholarship, a competitive and often socially biased endeavor. In April 1664, he secured the scholarship, possibly with help from his patron Humphrey Babington or Isaac Barrow, the Lucasian Professor of Mathematics. This scholarship granted Newton financial independence, allowing him to focus intensely on his investigations, often going without sleep or food.

3

Newton's Year of Wonders (1665-1666)

The Plague and Its Impact

In 1665, the plague hit England, forcing Newton to leave Cambridge. He spent the next eight months away, returning briefly in March 1666 before leaving again in June due to the plague's resurgence. He finally returned to Cambridge without interruption in April 1667, ready to continue his groundbreaking work.

> **Fun Fact:** During the plague years, Newton developed some of his most significant theories, including the laws of motion and universal gravitation, while isolated at Woolsthorpe.

In 1665, Isaac Newton was a promising student at the University of Cambridge, deeply engrossed in his studies of mathematics, optics, and natural philosophy. His academic progress was abruptly interrupted by an event that would change the course of history—the outbreak of the Great Plague.

The Great Plague of London was part of a series of bubonic plague outbreaks that swept through Europe during the 17th century. The plague, which reached its peak in 1665-1666, decimated the population of London, causing widespread panic and prompting authorities to take drastic measures to contain the spread of the disease. The University of Cambridge, like many institutions, closed its doors to protect its students and faculty.

NEWTON'S YEAR OF WONDERS (1665-1666)

Forced to leave Cambridge, Newton retreated to his family's estate, Woolsthorpe Manor, in Lincolnshire. This period, known as his "Annus Mirabilis" or "Year of Wonders," despite the grim backdrop of the plague, proved to be one of the most productive phases in Newton's life.

In the isolation of Woolsthorpe Manor, Newton's mind flourished. Deprived of formal education and academic resources, he relied on his intellect and curiosity to explore a range of scientific inquiries. This solitude allowed him to concentrate without the distractions and demands of university life, and it was during this time that he made some of his most significant discoveries.

The Great Plague 1665 by Rita Greer

One of the most famous legends surrounding Newton is his formulation of the law of universal gravitation. It is said that Newton observed an apple falling from a tree in the garden of Woolsthorpe Manor, which led him to ponder the forces at play. This moment of inspiration propelled him to develop his theories on gravity, culminating in the revolutionary idea that the same force governing the fall of the apple also governs the motion of the moon and the planets.

In addition to his work on gravity, Newton made groundbreaking advancements in mathematics during this period. He developed the fundamental principles of calculus, a mathematical framework that would become essential for understanding change and motion in both physics and engineering. Although his work on calculus was initially shared with only a few close colleagues, it eventually became a cornerstone of modern mathematics.

> **Fun Fact:** Newton invented calculus independently around the same time as Leibniz, leading to a famous dispute over who was the first to develop it.

Newton's investigations extended to optics as well. He conducted experiments with prisms, leading to his discovery that white light is composed of a spectrum of colors. This finding challenged the prevailing theories of light and color, laying the foundation for his later work, "Opticks," which would significantly influence the field of optical science.

The impact of the Great Plague on Newton's studies was profound. While the epidemic forced him into isolation, it also provided him with the uninterrupted time and space necessary to explore his ideas deeply. Newton's remarkable productivity during this period highlights the resilience and creativity that can emerge in the face of adversity.

Return to Woolsthorpe

**Woolsthorpe Manor in the pages of the book
Memoirs of Sir Isaac Newton's Life**

In 1665, the outbreak of the Great Plague forced the closure of Cambridge University, prompting Isaac Newton to return to his family home in Woolsthorpe. This period, spanning two years, became one of the most productive in Newton's life. Fifty years later, Newton would reminisce about these days, stating, "all of this was in the two plague years of 1665-66." He recalled being at the height of his creative potential, more engrossed in mathematics and philosophy than ever before or since.

During the two years that the university was closed due to the plague, Newton returned to his mother's house at Woolsthorpe.

Fifty years later, he recalled those days. After describing his work, he explained, "All of this was in the two plague years of 1665-66. For in those days I was in the prime of my age for invention and focused on Mathematics and Philosophy more than at any other time since."

From these remarks and similar ones made during the dispute over who invented calculus, the legend of Newton's "annus mirabilis" (year of wonders) was born. In reality, his achievements were likely the natural result of his existing efforts, which he could pursue more easily with the leisure time he had at Woolsthorpe. It is clear that during this period, Newton laid many foundations for his later work, and some conclusions he reached would not be published until 30 years later.

While working on mathematics, Newton began by listing 22 'problems' he wanted to investigate, grouped into five categories. He started with tangents to curves (differentiation) and the 'quadratures' of curves (areas under them, now known as integration). Using these new methods, he calculated the area under a hyperbola and developed ways to find the area under almost all known algebraic curves. In autumn 1665, he extended these ideas to consider areas swept out by moving points. He called these increments of area 'fluxionals,' marking the beginning of modern calculus. He saw 'velocity' as a fluxional, defined with respect to tiny time intervals, with time being an absolute quantity. He also discovered the relationship between integration and differentiation and, while summing various series expansions, found the 'binomial theorem.' In 1666, he returned to these mathematical questions and summarized his results in three papers. The last of these, written in October 1666, contains a full description of his theory of calculus. Newton also spent time on mechanics and optics.

Advances in Mechanics

In mechanics, he challenged Descartes' idea of an internal force of motion, instead arguing for external forces causing changes in motion. He realized that the momentum of two isolated bodies remains constant after collisions, leading to the principle of momentum conservation. Although he was close to finding his second law of motion, he was still confused about circular motion mechanics and temporarily agreed with Descartes that a body in circular motion strives to recede from the center, corresponding to a 'centrifugal' force. Newton calculated this force for circular motion and used his result to show that Earth's rotation doesn't fling bodies into the air because gravity is stronger than the centrifugal force. He also used Kepler's third law to suggest that gravitational force varies with the inverse square of the distance. However, it took another 30 years and several significant steps before he formulated his universal laws of motion.

During his time at Woolsthorpe, Newton also experimented with colors, inspired partly by Robert Hooke's "Micrographia" published in 1665. Hooke believed colors were a mixture of light and darkness and that light came in 'pulses.' Newton disagreed, noting that a white page with black writing viewed from a distance appears gray, not colored. Using prisms, he experimented with light, setting up an experiment where light traveled 22 feet from a window, through a prism, and projected a spectrum on the wall. He discovered that white light is composed of different colors, which the prism separated. His critical experiment, 'Experimentum Crucis,' involved passing a single color through a second prism, showing that the prism didn't change the color, proving that white light is a mixture of colors.

Newton's investigations into the colors of solid bodies were less successful. He believed these colors were produced by reflection, meaning a body appeared blue because it reflected blue light preferentially. He also examined Hooke's phenomenon of fine rings seen when curved glass contacts a flat piece, now known as 'Newton's rings.' Although he treated these rings quantitatively, he misunderstood them as vibrational disturbances in a medium of corpuscles making up light, rather than light pulses as Hooke suggested. From this time, Newton firmly believed light was made of particles.

> **Fun Fact:** During his time at Woolsthorpe, Newton's remarkable productivity and groundbreaking discoveries led to the legend of his annus mirabilis, or "year of wonders."

Advances in Optics

Newton's reflecting telescope, first made in 1668, finally brought him significant attention from the scientific community. He built it entirely by himself, including casting the mirror and creating specialized tools. This first telescope was only six inches long and one inch in diameter, but it magnified 40 times. He later made a more powerful one that could magnify up to 150 times. Proud of his invention, Newton showed it to others, and soon the Royal Society heard about it and requested to see it. When Barrow brought it to them at the end of 1671, it caused a sensation. Within a month, the news had reached Huyghens in Leiden, who was very impressed, and the Royal Society elected Newton as a member.

Newton, despite pretending not to care, was flattered. He shared the details of his telescope's operation and construction with Huyghens through letters. Finally, he sent his theory of colors to the Royal Society on February 6, 1672, which Oldenberg published in the Philosophical Transactions on February 19, 1672. Newton's description of his telescope appeared in the following issue.

The letter Newton sent included his research and experiments from his time at Woolsthorpe, showing how they led to the design of the telescope. This was the first time his work was open for discussion by other scientists. Most reactions were positive. However, some, like the French Jesuit Pardies, questioned if the recent discovery of diffraction by Grimaldi should be included in Newton's theory of light. Newton explained his scientific approach, stating that his work focused on the properties of light through experiments, not hypotheses.

Not everyone was supportive. Robert Hooke, a key figure at the Royal Society, saw optics as his field and rejected most of Newton's conclusions just a week after Newton's submission. Newton took four months to respond, during which he wrote a detailed exposition of his ideas on light but chose not to publish it. Instead, he responded to Hooke with a strong rebuttal in June. Following this, Newton became increasingly reluctant to respond to letters, although he did continue to correspond with Huyghens for a while. He even threatened to withdraw from the Royal Society and for years communicated directly only with Oldenberg and Collins.

Despite his reservations, Newton sent two manuscripts on optics to the Royal Society on December 7, 1678. One was titled "Discourse of Observations," and the other "An Hypothesis Explaining the Properties of Light Discoursed of in My Several Papers." In these, he reiterated his belief that light was made of particles guided by an aether. He explained refraction, reflection, and phenomena like 'Newton's rings' through variations in this aether. Newton also linked aether to gravitational force, suggesting that aether pressure influenced planetary motion and gravity. Even though he knew about the inverse square law of gravitation, Newton's ideas were still influenced by Cartesian concepts, far from his later theories. His deeper reasons for these views were rooted in his unpublished alchemical work.

> **Fun Fact:** Newton's experiments in optics led him to conclude that light is composed of particles, a belief he maintained despite the wave theory of light gaining prominence later.

Newton's Shift from Optics and Mechanics

Newton's attention shifted away from optics and mechanics for a considerable amount of time after the groundbreaking work he had done in the beginning. In spite of the fact that Leibniz had independently developed calculus by the year 1677, this shift in interest occurred. Newton spent the majority of his time between the years 1672 and 1684 working on theology and alchemy, two subjects that he considered to be fundamental questions.

Alchemy and Chemistry

Newton's work in the fields of chemistry and alchemy began at an early age. He had already made investments in ovens, glass equipment, and chemicals by the year 1669, which allowed him to begin his experiments. With the exception of a brief pause in the late 1680s, he carried on with this research for more than thirty years without a single interruption. The unpublished works that Newton produced during this time period reveal his profound interest in the principles of alchemy.

Newton's ideas on alchemy were first presented in his work on optics in the year 1678, specifically in his "Hypothesis Explaining the Properties of Light." He hypothesised the existence of a universal aether that was governed by active principles that governed behaviours such as gravity and phase changing. Through his work in alchemy, he sought to discover more profound explanations for phenomena such as magnetism and gravity, both of which were obviously not mechanical in nature.

> **Fun Fact:** Newton's alchemical experiments included a detailed study on the resistance of aether to pendulum motion. He found no discernible interaction between matter and aether, influencing his later rejection of the aether concept.

Theological Pursuits

At the beginning of the 1670s, Newton's interest in theology began to emerge, and by 1674, he had become heavily involved in the field. His theological ideas were revolutionary, and they posed a challenge to the fundamental beliefs held by the Anglican Church. The victory of Athanasius over Arius, which occurred in the fourth century, led Newton to the conclusion that

John Locke

Christianity had been corrupted since that time. He was of the opinion that genuine religion existed prior to the occurrence of this corruption, and that all of the ancient gods were, in essence, the same deity, albeit represented by different names.

Newton became an Arian as a result of his theological research; however, he did not disclose his beliefs to anyone outside of his immediate circle of acquaintances, including, for example, the philosopher John Locke. His pursuit of philosophical truth led him to pursue theological studies, which was a natural extension of his pursuit.

Fun Fact: Newton managed to avoid expulsion from Trinity College by receiving a royal dispensation in 1675, exempting him from taking Holy Orders, which was usually required for fellows of the college.

By understanding these diverse interests, we gain a fuller picture of Newton's relentless pursuit of knowledge and his impact on multiple fields beyond just physics and mathematics.

4

Return to Cambridge and Academic Career

Fellowship and Professorship at Cambridge

Isaac Newton's tenure at the University of Cambridge marked a transformative period in his career and the history of science. His roles as a fellow and later as the Lucasian Professor of Mathematics provided him with the platform and resources to develop his groundbreaking theories in mathematics, physics, and optics.

Fellowship at Trinity College

In 1667, Newton returned to Cambridge after the Great Plague of London had forced the university to close temporarily. He was elected a fellow of Trinity College, a position that offered him financial stability and the freedom to pursue his research. This fellowship was crucial as it provided Newton with the time and resources needed to delve into his scientific inquiries.

Research and Discoveries

During his early years as a fellow, Newton made significant progress in several areas:

- **Mathematics:** He refined his methods of calculus, which he referred to as "the method of fluxions." This work laid the foundation for modern calculus.
- **Optics:** Newton conducted experiments that led to his theory of light and color. He demonstrated that white light is composed of a spectrum of colors, which could be separated by a prism and then recombined. This challenged the prevailing theories of light and color and was a major contribution to the field of optics.

Lucasian Professorship

In 1669, Newton was appointed the Lucasian Professor of Mathematics at Cambridge, succeeding Isaac Barrow. At just 26 years old, Newton took on this prestigious role, which significantly boosted his academic standing and influence.

Mathematical Contributions

As Lucasian Professor, Newton continued to advance his work in mathematics. He systematically developed his calculus, addressing problems involving motion and change. Although his work remained largely unpublished at this time, his methods would later revolutionize mathematics.

Optical Research

Newton's tenure as Lucasian Professor saw the publication of his first major scientific work, "New Theory about Light and Colors," in 1672. Presented to the Royal Society, this paper detailed his experiments with prisms and his conclusions about the nature of light. His findings laid the groundwork for his later book, "Opticks," published in 1704.

Newton's Optical Instrument

The PRINCIPIA: DAWN OF NEWTONIAN MECHANICS

Early Life and Interests

Isaac Newton, known for his groundbreaking work in physics, spent many years deeply immersed in the study of theology and alchemy. During the late 1670s and early 1680s, he was particularly interested in developing a theory that could explain the known phenomena of mechanics, optics, and chemistry through non-mechanical means. He focused on the concept of an aether, which he believed had hidden properties that could provide such explanations. However, Newton never shared or published this work, leading to a lack of recognition for these studies.

A Twist of Fate

In the years 1680-1684, a series of events dramatically changed the direction of Newton's research. These events led him to abandon his previous ideas and embark on a new path that resulted in the creation of a revolutionary system of mechanics. This new theory was devoid of any aether and was later published as the "Philosophiae Naturalis Principia Mathematica" ('The Mathematical Principles of Natural Philosophy') in 1687. This work is considered one of the most crucial developments in the history of science.

Observations and Realizations

In 1680, a spectacular comet appeared, followed by another in 1682 (later identified as Halley's Comet). Newton's observations of these comets led him to realize that cometary dynamics could be understood similarly to planetary motion. This was a significant step towards his idea of universal gravitation, which proposed that all celestial bodies were governed by the same principles.

Key Discussion at the Royal Society

In January 1684, Edmund Halley, Robert Hooke, and Christopher Wren had a pivotal discussion about celestial mechanics. Hooke claimed he could demonstrate all celestial dynamics starting from an inverse square attraction but did not reveal his proof. Halley later visited Newton and asked him about the motion of an object in such a force field. Newton immediately responded that it would be an ellipse, which he had calculated previously. This exchange spurred Newton to elaborate on his notes and led to the creation of a nine-page manuscript demonstrating that a $1/r^2$ attraction would lead to motion along a conic section.

Writing of the Principia

From August 1684 to the spring of 1686, Newton dedicated himself to refining his ideas and formulating a comprehensive system of mechanics. Encouraged and supported by Halley, Newton expanded his original manuscript into a detailed and rigorous work. This process involved multiple revisions and the development of new concepts, such as centripetal forces and the laws of motion.

Philosophical Underpinnings

Newton's philosophical endeavor aimed to establish a framework in which all dynamics could be derived. He introduced the idea of absolute space and time, which, although no longer used in modern physics, were crucial to his formulations. He also struggled with the concept of inherent force, which eventually led to his first law of motion. Over time, Newton abandoned the idea of an aether and embraced the concept of forces acting at a distance through a vacuum.

The Laws of Motion

Newton's first law states that a body at rest or moving uniformly in a straight line will remain in that state unless acted upon by an external force. His second law defines the relationship between force, mass, and acceleration, and his third law states that for every action, there is an equal and opposite reaction. These laws formed the foundation of classical mechanics and revolutionized the understanding of motion and forces.

Universal Gravitation

Newton's hypothesis of universal gravitation emerged from his understanding of planetary motions and pendulum experiments. He proposed that all massive bodies exert a gravitational force proportional to their mass and inversely proportional to the square of the distance between them. This idea explained the motion of celestial bodies and provided a unified framework for understanding gravity.

Key Contributions in the Principia

Newton's Principia addressed several crucial problems, including:
- The gravitational attraction exerted by a sphere of uniform density.

- The mutual perturbations of planets and their effects on orbits.
- The stability of orbits and the laws governing elliptical motion.
- The effects of tides and the precession of the Earth's axis.
- The complex dynamics of the moon's orbit and its interactions with the Earth and the sun.
- The motion of fluids and the propagation of disturbances in fluids and elastic media.
- The instability of vortex motion and its implications for Cartesian theories.

Publication and Legacy

By November 1685, Newton had completed the first two books of the Principia. Despite financial difficulties and disputes with Hooke, Halley's determination ensured the work's publication. The Principia was printed in 1687 and had a profound impact on the scientific community. Its rigorous mathematical approach and comprehensive treatment of mechanics and gravitation laid the groundwork for modern physics.

Fun Fact: Newton's Principia was so mathematically dense and complex that only a handful of people in his time fully understood it. One of those was Edmond Halley, who not only encouraged and supported Newton but also funded the publication of the Principia, despite the Royal Society's financial troubles.

Debates and Controversies with Contemporaries

1. The Hooke Controversy

Isaac Newton's career was characterized not only by his revolutionary scientific discoveries but also by intense conflicts with his contemporaries. One of the most notable and enduring disputes was with Robert Hooke, a polymath and a prominent figure in the Royal Society.

Introduction to Robert Hooke

Robert Hooke

Robert Hooke (1635–1703) was a versatile scientist, architect, and inventor, known for his contributions to biology, physics, and astronomy. He was appointed Curator of Experiments for the Royal Society, where he became a key figure alongside Newton.

The Dispute Over Light and Color

One of the earliest points of contention between Newton and Hooke arose from Newton's experiments with light and color. Newton conducted experiments with prisms that demonstrated that white light could be split into a spectrum of colors. This led to his groundbreaking theory that white light is composed of different colors and that each color is refracted at different angles due to its wavelength.

Hooke criticized Newton's theory, arguing instead for a wave theory of light. He disputed Newton's methodology and conclusions, suggesting alternative explanations for the phenomenon of colors in light. This disagreement laid the foundation for a prolonged and bitter rivalry between the two scientists.

Hooke's Challenge on Gravity

Another source of conflict stemmed from Hooke's claims regarding the theory of gravitation. Hooke contended that he had already developed a theory of gravity before Newton, albeit in a more rudimentary form. In 1679, Hooke wrote to Newton, suggesting that the inverse-square law of gravity might explain Kepler's laws of planetary motion. This correspondence prompted Newton to delve deeper into his studies on gravity, eventually leading to the publication of his seminal work, "Philosophiæ Naturalis Principia Mathematica," commonly known as the "Principia Mathematica."

Personal and Professional Clashes

Beyond their scientific disagreements, Newton and Hooke's relationship was marked by personal animosity and professional clashes. Hooke was known for his sharp wit and critical nature, which often exacerbated tensions with Newton. The rivalry extended beyond scientific debate to personal attacks and disputes over credit for discoveries.

Their interactions within the Royal Society and other scientific circles were fraught with tension, affecting their respective reputations and contributions to science. Newton, often reclusive and sensitive to criticism, responded fiercely to challenges from Hooke and others, leading to a legacy of strained relationships and unresolved disputes.

2. The Leibniz Controversy

Isaac Newton's legacy in mathematics and science is also intertwined with a contentious dispute with Gottfried Wilhelm Leibniz, a prominent German mathematician and philosopher of the 17th century.

Introduction to Gottfried Wilhelm Leibniz

Leibniz

Gottfried Wilhelm Leibniz (1646–1716) was a polymath known for his contributions to mathematics, philosophy, and numerous other fields. He independently developed a system of differential and integral calculus, which he published in 1684, predating Newton's formal publication.

The Calculus Priority Dispute

The heart of the dispute between Newton and Leibniz revolved around the invention of calculus. Newton had developed his method of fluxions in the mid-1660s as a mathematical tool to study rates of change and accumulation, but he did not publish his work until later. Meanwhile, Leibniz formulated his own version of calculus, based on different principles, and published his findings in 1684.

When Newton's "Principia Mathematica" was published in 1687, it included a section on calculus that showcased his method of fluxions. This publication ignited a controversy over who had truly invented calculus first—Newton or Leibniz. Each side had supporters and detractors within the scientific community, leading to a heated debate that persisted for decades.

Accusations of Plagiarism

Accusations of plagiarism were hurled from both sides. Newton's supporters argued that Leibniz had borrowed heavily from Newton's unpublished manuscripts or had been influenced by them indirectly. Conversely, Leibniz and his supporters claimed that Newton had known about Leibniz's work before publishing his own calculus methods and had incorporated some of Leibniz's ideas without credit.

These accusations of intellectual theft further fueled the animosity between the two camps, contributing to a climate of distrust and rivalry.

Impact on European Science

The Newton-Leibniz controversy had profound implications for European science and mathematics. It polarized the mathematical community, with many mathematicians and scientists taking sides either with Newton or with Leibniz. This polarization influenced the development of mathematical notations and techniques, as adherents of each mathematician's method sought to defend and promote their preferred approach.

Despite the acrimony, both Newton's and Leibniz's contributions to calculus laid the foundation for modern mathematics. Their respective methods and notations coalesced over time into what is now known as the differential and integral calculus, forming an essential part of higher mathematics and scientific inquiry.

Conflicts with Flamsteed

Isaac Newton's career was marked by not only scientific brilliance but also by conflicts with contemporaries, including John Flamsteed, the Astronomer Royal of England.

3. *John Flamsteed, the Astronomer Royal*

John Flamsteed (1646–1719) was appointed as the first Astronomer Royal by King Charles II in 1675. His primary task was to accurately observe and catalog the positions of celestial objects, a monumental undertaking that laid the foundation for modern astronomy.

Disagreement Over Data Access

John Flamsteed

Newton, always eager to expand his knowledge of celestial mechanics and gravitational theory, sought access to Flamsteed's meticulously recorded astronomical data. Flamsteed, however, was protective of his observations and reluctant to share them with Newton, whom he viewed as a colleague but also as someone who might exploit or misinterpret his work.

This disagreement over access to data became a point of contention between Newton and Flamsteed. Newton believed that access to Flamsteed's data was crucial for his research, especially in verifying and refining his theories of celestial motion and gravitational attraction.

Publication Controversy

Tensions reached a breaking point when Newton, frustrated by Flamsteed's reluctance to share data and by what he perceived as Flamsteed's slow progress in publishing his catalog of star positions, took matters into his own hands. In 1696, without Flamsteed's consent, Newton arranged for the publication of Flamsteed's incomplete star catalog as part of the "Historia Coelestis Britannica" (British Celestial History).

Flamsteed was outraged by this unauthorized publication, seeing it as a breach of trust and a violation of his intellectual property rights. The publication controversy strained Newton and Flamsteed's relationship even further, leading to years of acrimony and legal battles.

Resolution and Legacy

Ultimately, Flamsteed continued his astronomical observations and eventually published his complete star catalog in 1725, posthumously. The feud with Newton left a lasting impact on Flamsteed, influencing his attitudes toward collaboration and data sharing within the scientific community.

For Newton, the conflict with Flamsteed was part of a pattern of contentious relationships with his contemporaries, driven by his relentless pursuit of knowledge and his sometimes uncompromising demeanor. Despite the conflicts, Newton's contributions to astronomy and celestial mechanics remained foundational, shaping the course of scientific inquiry for centuries to come.

4. Relationship with Edmund Halley

Isaac Newton's career was marked not only by conflicts but also by fruitful collaborations, none more notable than his relationship with Edmund Halley, a fellow scientist and supporter.

Collaborative Efforts

Despite Newton's often contentious relationships with his contemporaries, he shared a notably productive and supportive relationship with Edmund Halley (1656–1742). Halley, an English astronomer and mathematician, is best known for calculating the orbit of the comet that now bears his name, Halley's Comet.

Halley recognized the genius in Newton's work early on and became an ardent supporter of Newton's

Edmund Halley

theories and research. Despite their occasional disagreements, Halley and Newton collaborated on several important scientific endeavors.

Halley's Support of the Principia

One of the most crucial aspects of their relationship was Halley's support for the publication of Newton's magnum opus, the "Philosophiæ Naturalis Principia Mathematica" (Mathematical Principles of Natural Philosophy). Newton had been working on his theories of motion and universal gravitation for years, but it was Halley who played a pivotal role in bringing Newton's work to publication.

In 1684, Halley visited Newton to discuss the laws of planetary motion. Impressed by Newton's explanations, Halley encouraged him to develop his ideas into a comprehensive treatise. Halley's financial support and personal advocacy were instrumental in persuading Newton to publish his groundbreaking work on celestial mechanics.

Halley not only championed Newton's theories but also undertook the task of editing and preparing the "Principia" for publication. He bore the financial costs of printing the book himself when the Royal Society hesitated to finance it fully.

Legacy and Impact

The collaboration between Newton and Halley exemplifies how supportive relationships can foster groundbreaking scientific advancements. Halley's role in supporting and promoting Newton's work ensured that the "Principia Mathematica" became one of the most influential works in the history of science, revolutionizing our understanding of the laws governing the universe.

Their relationship also underscores the importance of collaboration and mentorship in scientific progress, demonstrating how scientists can work together to advance knowledge and shape the course of scientific inquiry for generations to come.

Contribution to Mathematics, Optics, and Physics

1. Contributions to Mathematics

Isaac Newton's contributions to mathematics were profound and laid the groundwork for many branches of modern mathematics.

Development of Calculus

In the mid-1660s, Newton developed a new mathematical method he called "method of fluxions," which is now known as differential calculus. This revolutionary approach allowed for the calculation of instantaneous rates of change and the determination of slopes of curves at any point. Newton used fluxions to solve problems in physics and astronomy, particularly in his studies of planetary motion and gravitational theory.

The essence of Newton's calculus lies in his concept of fluxions, where he considered quantities changing continuously with time. This concept enabled him to formulate mathematical expressions for rates of change, leading to the fundamental theorem of calculus, which states the relationship between differentiation and integration.

Binomial Theorem

Newton made significant advancements in algebra, particularly with his generalization of the binomial theorem. The binomial theorem, which states the expansion of powers of a binomial, had been known in various forms before Newton. However, Newton provided a systematic method for expanding any power of a binomial, laying the foundation for algebraic manipulations and combinatorial mathematics.

Newton's formulation of the binomial theorem allowed for the efficient calculation of polynomial expansions and contributed to the development of algebraic techniques that are still used extensively in mathematics today.

Mathematical Contributions Beyond Calculus

Isaac Newton's contributions to mathematics extended far beyond his groundbreaking work on calculus. His work on various mathematical problems and theories significantly advanced the fields of geometry and algebra. Additionally, Newton's influence on the development of mathematical notation and practice has had a lasting impact on the discipline. This chapter explores Newton's broader mathematical contributions, highlighting his work in geometry, algebra, and his enduring influence on mathematical practice.

Newton's Work on Mathematical Problems and Theories

1. *Contributions to Geometry:*

- **Synthetic Geometry:** Newton made significant contributions to synthetic geometry, the study of geometry using classical constructions and properties without the use of coordinates. He focused on the properties and relationships of geometric figures, emphasizing the importance of logical reasoning and rigorous proofs.
- **Conic Sections:** Newton's work on conic sections—ellipse, parabola, and hyperbola—was notable. He studied their properties and applications, particularly in the context of

celestial mechanics. His analysis of the orbits of planets and comets, which he modeled as conic sections, was a crucial aspect of his work in "Principia Mathematica."
- **Geometric Transformations:** Newton explored geometric transformations, such as translations, rotations, and reflections. His insights into these transformations helped lay the groundwork for later developments in projective geometry and group theory.

2. Advances in Algebra:

- **Polynomial Equations:** Newton made substantial contributions to the study of polynomial equations. He developed methods for finding roots of polynomials, including the use of iterative techniques that anticipated modern numerical analysis methods. Newton's method for approximating roots of a polynomial, known as the Newton-Raphson method, remains a fundamental algorithm in numerical mathematics.
- **Binomial Theorem:** Newton generalized the binomial theorem to apply to any real exponent, not just positive integers. His formulation of the binomial expansion for non-integer powers was a significant advancement in algebra and provided a powerful tool for mathematical analysis.
- **Algebraic Notation:** Newton's work contributed to the standardization and refinement of algebraic notation. He used symbols and operations that became more widely adopted in mathematical practice, helping to clarify and simplify complex algebraic expressions.

Newton's Influence on Mathematical Notation and Practice

1. Development of Notation:

- **Fluxions and Fluents:** In his work on calculus, Newton introduced the concepts of fluxions and fluents, which correspond to derivatives and integrals in modern notation. Although Leibniz's notation for calculus eventually became more popular, Newton's terminology influenced the development of mathematical notation and concepts.
- **Symbolic Notation:** Newton's use of symbolic notation in algebra and geometry helped to formalize mathematical expressions and operations. His approach to notation made mathematical arguments more precise and easier to communicate, laying the groundwork for modern symbolic algebra.

2. Mathematical Practice and Methodology:

- **Analytical Methods:** Newton's analytical methods, which combined algebraic techniques with geometric reasoning, influenced the development of mathematical practice. His emphasis on the interplay between algebra and geometry helped to bridge the gap between these two areas of mathematics.
- **Iterative Techniques:** Newton's iterative techniques for solving equations, such as the Newton-Raphson method, exemplified his approach to mathematical problem-solving. These techniques emphasized the importance of approximation and convergence, concepts that are central to modern numerical analysis.

3. Influence on Later Mathematicians:

- **Direct Influence:** Newton's work directly influenced many of his contemporaries and successors. Mathematicians such as John Wallis, Roger Cotes, and Brook Taylor built upon Newton's methods and ideas, further advancing the fields of algebra and geometry.
- **Long-Term Impact:** Newton's contributions had a lasting impact on the development of mathematics. His methods and approaches became foundational principles that guided mathematical research and education for centuries. The influence of his work can be seen in the development of mathematical analysis, numerical methods, and the formalization of mathematical theory.

Notable Works and Publications

1. *Arithmetica Universalis (Universal Arithmetic):*

- Newton's "Arithmetica Universalis," published posthumously in 1707, was a comprehensive treatise on algebra. The book covered topics such as the theory of equations, the binomial theorem, and the arithmetic of irrational numbers. It became a standard reference in algebra and influenced subsequent generations of mathematicians.

2. *Geometria Analytica (Analytical Geometry):*

- Although not published as a standalone work, Newton's contributions to analytical geometry were significant. His methods for analyzing geometric problems using algebraic techniques were integrated into his broader body of work and influenced the development of the field.

Arithmetica Universalis

3. Contributions to Optics

Isaac Newton's contributions to optics were groundbreaking and laid the foundation for our modern understanding of light and its properties.

Theory of Light and Color

Newton's experiments with prisms in the late 1660s demonstrated that white light is composed of a spectrum of colors. He passed a beam of sunlight through a glass prism and observed the separation of light into its constituent colors: red, orange, yellow, green, blue, indigo, and violet. This experiment led Newton to propose that each color is refracted at different angles due to its wavelength, thereby revealing the spectrum of visible light.

Newton's findings were published in his seminal work "Opticks" in 1704. In this book, he articulated his theory that white light is a mixture of all colors and that each color corresponds to a specific wavelength of light. His theory of light laid the groundwork for the wave theory of light and later developments in optics and electromagnetic theory.

Reflecting Telescope

To address the problem of chromatic aberration in traditional refracting telescopes (where lenses refract different colors of light at different angles, leading to color distortion), Newton developed the first practical reflecting telescope in 1668. Instead of using lenses to gather and focus light, Newton's reflecting telescope used a curved mirror to reflect and converge light onto a focal point.

Newton's Reflecting Telescope

Newton's reflecting telescope was a significant improvement over refracting telescopes of the time. It provided clearer and sharper images without the color distortions caused by lenses. This innovation revolutionized observational astronomy and led to the development of larger and more powerful telescopes that could observe distant celestial objects with greater precision.

Corpuscular Theory of Light

Newton proposed a theory that light consists of particles or corpuscles. According to his corpuscular theory of light, these particles travel in straight lines and exhibit properties such as reflection and refraction. Newton's corpuscular theory contrasted with the prevailing wave theory of light advocated by Christiaan Huygens and later Thomas Young.

Christiaan Huygens

Thomas Young

Newton's corpuscular theory dominated scientific thought for much of the 18th century until the wave theory gained prominence with the work of Augustin-Jean Fresnel and others in the 19th century. Despite its eventual displacement by wave theory, Newton's corpuscular theory contributed to the understanding of light as discrete particles and influenced later developments in quantum mechanics and particle physics.

Legacy and Impact

Isaac Newton's contributions to optics fundamentally transformed our understanding of light, color, and the nature of vision. His experiments with prisms and development of the reflecting telescope advanced observational astronomy and laid the groundwork for modern optical technologies. Newton's corpuscular theory of light, while eventually supplanted by wave theory, contributed to the evolution of scientific inquiry and the exploration of light's dual particle-wave nature.

4. Contributions to Physics

Isaac Newton's contributions to physics revolutionized our understanding of motion, gravitation, and the fundamental laws governing the universe.

Laws of Motion

Newton formulated the three fundamental laws of motion, which are foundational principles in classical mechanics:

1. **First Law (Law of Inertia)**: An object at rest will remain at rest, and an object in motion will continue in motion with constant velocity unless acted upon by an external force.
2. **Second Law (Law of Acceleration)**: The acceleration of an object is directly proportional to the force acting upon it and inversely proportional to its mass. This law is mathematically expressed as $F=maF = maF=ma$, where FFF is the force applied, mmm is the mass of the object, and aaa is its acceleration.
3. **Third Law (Action and Reaction)**: For every action, there is an equal and opposite reaction. This law explains the reciprocal nature of forces between interacting objects.

Newton's laws of motion provided a comprehensive framework for understanding how forces influence the motion of objects, from the smallest particles to celestial bodies, and laid the groundwork for classical mechanics.

Law of Universal Gravitation

Newton proposed the law of universal gravitation, which states that every mass in the universe attracts every other mass with a force proportional to the product of their masses and inversely proportional to the square of the distance between their centers. Mathematically, this is expressed as:

PHILOSOPHIÆ NATURALIS PRINCIPIA MATHEMATICA.

Autore JS. NEWTON, Trin. Coll. Cantab. Soc. Matheseos Professore Lucasiano, & Societatis Regalis Sodali.

IMPRIMATUR·
S. PEPYS, Reg. Soc. PRÆSES.
Julii 5. 1686.

LONDINI,
Jussu Societatis Regiæ ac Typis Josephi Streater. Prostat apud plures Bibliopolas. Anno MDCLXXXVII.

Mathematical Principles of Natural Philosophy

$$F = G\frac{m_1 m_2}{r^2}$$

where F is the gravitational force between two masses m_1 and m_2, r is the distance between their centers, and G is the gravitational constant.

Newton's law of universal gravitation provided a unified explanation for the motion of celestial bodies, such as planets and moons, and is instrumental in understanding the dynamics of the solar system and beyond.

Principia Mathematica

Published in 1687, Newton's "Philosophiæ Naturalis Principia Mathematica" (Mathematical Principles of Natural Philosophy) is one of the most influential works in the history of science. In this monumental work, Newton not only articulated his laws of motion and universal gravitation but also provided a mathematical framework for understanding the mechanics of celestial bodies.

The "Principia" introduced the concept of mathematical modeling to describe the motion of objects under the influence of gravitational forces. Newton's mathematical formulations and rigorous approach to scientific inquiry laid the foundation for modern physics and set a standard for scientific methodology.

Advances in Mechanics and Fluid Dynamics

Newton made significant contributions to mechanics beyond his laws of motion and gravitation. He studied the motion of fluids and developed principles of fluid dynamics that laid the groundwork for understanding how fluids, such as water and air, behave under different conditions. His insights into fluid motion and resistance were crucial for advancements in engineering, hydrodynamics, and aerodynamics.

In addition to fluid dynamics, Newton's studies of rigid bodies and their motion contributed to the development of classical mechanics. His work on the equilibrium and motion of objects provided practical insights into the design and construction of mechanical systems, influencing fields such as engineering and architecture.

Legacy and Impact

Isaac Newton's contributions to physics transformed our understanding of the natural world and laid the foundation for classical mechanics, gravitational theory, and fluid dynamics. His laws of motion and universal gravitation provided a framework for scientific inquiry that continues to shape our understanding of physical phenomena and inspire new discoveries in physics and engineering.

Newton's "Principia Mathematica" remains a cornerstone of scientific literature, demonstrating the power of mathematical reasoning and empirical observation in advancing knowledge. His legacy as a physicist and mathematician continues to influence diverse fields of study, reaffirming his status as one of the greatest scientific minds in history.

5

Later Career and Public Service (1696-1727)

The latter part of Isaac Newton's career was characterized by significant accomplishments in public service and administrative roles. These accomplishments allowed him to extend his influence beyond the realm of science and into the realms of politics and practicality in England during the 17th and 18th centuries.

Move to London and Appointment as Warden of the Mint

In 1696, Isaac Newton embarked on a new phase of his illustrious career, transitioning from the academic world of Cambridge to the bustling administrative center of London. This move marked the beginning of his significant contributions to public service, most notably through his appointment as Warden of the Royal Mint.

Background and Appointment

Isaac Newton's move to London and his appointment as Warden of the Royal Mint were orchestrated by Charles Montagu, the Chancellor of the Exchequer and a strong admirer of Newton's scientific achievements. Montagu, recognizing Newton's analytical prowess and reputation for integrity, saw him as an ideal candidate to tackle the challenges facing England's currency system. The offer was also a strategic opportunity for Newton, who had been experiencing personal and professional challenges at Cambridge, including disputes with fellow academics and waning interest in his scientific work.

The Royal Mint

Responsibilities as Warden

As Warden of the Mint, Newton's primary responsibilities included overseeing the production of currency, ensuring its quality, and combating the widespread issue of counterfeiting. The position, though nominally administrative, required a keen understanding of economics, metallurgy, and law. Newton's role was critical, especially during a period of significant monetary reform in England.

One of Newton's first tasks was to address the rampant

counterfeiting and clipping of coins. Counterfeiters would shave off small amounts of precious metal from coins and then pass them off as full value. This practice had led to a substantial degradation of the currency, undermining public confidence and economic stability.

His Move to London

Newton's relocation to London was a major life change. He settled in a house provided by the Mint in the Tower of London, a secure and central location for his new role. This move not only symbolized a geographical shift but also a transition in the focus of his professional endeavors. In London, Newton was at the heart of political and financial power, which provided him with new opportunities and challenges.

Newton's tenure as Warden of the Mint was highly successful. His reforms restored the integrity of the English currency system, stabilized the economy, and regained public confidence in the nation's money. His analytical skills, combined with his commitment to public service, ensured the successful implementation of these critical reforms.

Newton's work at the Mint exemplified his ability to apply scientific thinking to practical problems, demonstrating his versatility and broadening the scope of his contributions beyond pure science. His success in this role led to his promotion to Master of the Mint in 1699, a position he held until his death in 1727.

Reformation of England's Coinage System

Isaac Newton's tenure at the Royal Mint coincided with a period of significant monetary instability in England. His role in the reformation of the coinage system was instrumental in restoring confidence in the nation's currency and stabilizing the economy. Newton's scientific approach and meticulous attention to detail made him uniquely suited to tackle the challenges of the Great Recoinage.

A William and Mary Guinea Minted under Isaac Newton

The Context of the Recoinage

By the late 17th century, England's coinage was in a state of crisis. The currency system was plagued by widespread clipping and counterfeiting, practices that had severely debased the value of coins in circulation. Clipping involved shaving off small amounts of precious metal from the edges of coins, which were then passed off at full face value. Counterfeiting was also rampant, with fake coins undermining the integrity of the currency.

The economy was suffering as a result, with a lack of public confidence in the coinage leading to hoarding of good coins and reluctance to use debased ones. The Great Recoinage of 1696 was initiated as a response to this crisis, aiming to replace the old, clipped, and counterfeit coins with newly minted ones of standard weight and purity.

Newton's Initial Challenges

In 1696, Isaac Newton was appointed Warden of the Royal Mint, a position that placed him at the forefront of the recoinage effort. Newton's appointment was part of a broader strategy to leverage his analytical skills and reputation for integrity to restore the currency system.

Upon taking up his position, Newton faced several immediate challenges:

- **Assessing the Extent of the Problem**: Newton had to understand the full scope of clipping and counterfeiting to develop effective countermeasures.
- **Improving Mint Operations**: The existing processes at the Mint were inefficient and incapable of producing the high volume of new coins required.
- **Restoring Public Trust**: Newton needed to ensure that the new coinage would be trusted by the public, requiring visible improvements in coin quality and security.

Key Reforms Implemented by Newton

Newton's approach to the reformation of England's coinage system was methodical and comprehensive. His reforms addressed both the technical aspects of coin production and the legal framework needed to deter and punish counterfeiters.

1. **Introduction of Milled Edges**: One of Newton's most significant technical innovations was the introduction of milled edges on coins. This design feature made it

immediately apparent if a coin had been clipped, as the absence of the milled edge would indicate tampering. This simple yet effective measure greatly reduced the practice of clipping.

2. **Improvement of Coin Quality**: Newton implemented rigorous standards for the weight and purity of the metal used in coinage. He ensured that each coin met exacting specifications, which helped restore confidence in the currency. Newton's scientific background enabled him to oversee the production process with precision, reducing variability and increasing the overall quality of the coins.

3. **Efficient Minting Processes**: To meet the high demand for new coins, Newton reorganized the Mint's operations, introducing new machinery and processes to increase efficiency. He utilized advancements in metallurgy and mechanics to streamline production, allowing the Mint to produce large quantities of high-quality coins rapidly.

4. **Prosecution of Counterfeiters**: Newton took a proactive approach to law enforcement, rigorously investigating and prosecuting counterfeiters. He gathered evidence meticulously and used his legal authority to bring counterfeiters to trial. His efforts resulted in numerous convictions, which served as a deterrent to others and helped curb the spread of counterfeit coins.

5. **Public Communication**: Understanding the importance of public confidence, Newton ensured that the public was well-informed about the new coinage. He communicated the benefits of the new, more secure coins and the efforts being made to eliminate counterfeit currency. This transparency helped rebuild trust in the monetary system.

Impact

Newton's reforms had a profound and lasting impact on England's economy. The successful recoinage restored public confidence in the currency, stabilized the economy, and provided a sound basis for future economic growth. The introduction of milled edges and improvements in coin quality became standard practices in minting, influencing coinage systems worldwide.

Newton's work at the Mint also demonstrated the application of scientific principles to practical and administrative challenges, showcasing his versatility and ability to apply his intellect beyond theoretical pursuits. His tenure as Warden, and later as Master of the Mint, highlighted his dedication to public service and his capability as an administrator and reformer.

Isaac Newton's contributions to the reformation of England's coinage system stand as a testament to his remarkable ability to combine scientific rigor with practical problem-solving, leaving an enduring legacy in both the scientific and economic history of England.

Newton's contributions to the Royal Mint had lasting effects, setting high standards for currency production and integrity. His work laid the groundwork for modern practices in coinage and monetary policy, underscoring his legacy as a polymath who not only transformed science but also significantly influenced the economic stability of his country.

Presidency of the Royal Society

Isaac Newton's election as President of the Royal Society in 1703 marked the beginning of a significant period in the history of this prestigious scientific institution. Newton's leadership profoundly influenced the direction of scientific research and the development of the Royal Society, solidifying its status as a leading organization dedicated to the advancement of knowledge.

Background and Election

The Royal Society, founded in 1660, had established itself as a hub for scientific inquiry and innovation. By the early 18th century, it was recognized as one of the foremost scientific institutions in Europe. Newton's election as President came at a time when the Society was looking to strengthen its influence and expand its contributions to the scientific community.

Newton was elected President following the death of Sir Hans Sloane, the previous president. His reputation as one of the greatest scientists of his era, primarily due to his groundbreaking work in physics and mathematics, made him a natural choice for the position. Newton's presidency was characterized by his efforts to promote rigorous scientific research, foster collaboration among scientists, and enhance the Society's role in disseminating scientific knowledge.

Key Initiatives and Contributions

1. **Promotion of Scientific Research**: Newton's tenure as President saw a renewed emphasis on empirical research and experimentation. He encouraged members of the Royal Society to conduct detailed experiments and publish their findings, thereby contributing to the collective scientific knowledge. Under his leadership, the Society supported a wide range of scientific endeavors, from astronomy and physics to biology and chemistry.
2. **Support for Publication**: One of Newton's significant contributions was his support for the publication of scientific

works. He recognized the importance of disseminating scientific knowledge widely and ensured that the Royal Society's journal, the "Philosophical Transactions," continued to publish high-quality research. Newton himself contributed to the journal, sharing his own discoveries and encouraging others to do the same.

3. **Mentorship and Collaboration**: Newton's presidency was marked by his mentorship of younger scientists and his efforts to foster a collaborative environment within the Society. He provided guidance and support to emerging scientists, helping to nurture the next generation of scientific leaders. Newton's influence and encouragement were instrumental in advancing the careers of many notable scientists of the time.

4. **Institutional Strengthening**: Newton worked to strengthen the administrative and financial foundations of the Royal Society. He implemented reforms to improve the Society's governance, ensuring that it operated efficiently and effectively. Newton's administrative acumen helped secure funding and resources necessary for the Society's activities, enabling it to expand its reach and impact.

Newton's presidency of the Royal Society had a lasting impact on the institution and the broader scientific community. His emphasis on rigorous research, publication, and collaboration set high standards for scientific practice and contributed to the Society's reputation as a leading center for scientific excellence.

Under Newton's leadership, the Royal Society made significant strides in advancing scientific knowledge and promoting the application of scientific principles to practical problems. His support for emerging scientists and his commitment to public engagement helped inspire a new generation of researchers and fostered a culture of scientific inquiry that persisted long after his presidency.

Newton's tenure also solidified the Royal Society's role as a key player in the global scientific community. The Society's journal, the "Philosophical Transactions," became an essential platform for the dissemination of scientific research, influencing scientific thought and development worldwide.

Isaac Newton's presidency of the Royal Society was a period of significant growth and achievement for the institution. His leadership, vision, and commitment to scientific rigor left an indelible mark on the Society and the field of science as a whole. Newton's contributions as President extended his influence beyond his own scientific discoveries, shaping the direction of scientific research and fostering a legacy of excellence and innovation that continues to inspire scientists today.

Political and Administrative Roles

Isaac Newton's later career extended beyond his scientific achievements into significant political and administrative roles. His contributions in these areas demonstrated his versatility and commitment to public service, influencing both the governance of scientific institutions and the broader political landscape of England.

Member of Parliament

Isaac Newton served as a Member of Parliament (MP) for the University of Cambridge in two separate terms: from 1689 to 1690 and again from 1701 to 1702. Although his contributions to parliamentary debates were limited and he is often remembered for his silence in the House of Commons, his election to this position was significant for several reasons:

1. **Representation of Academic Interests**: Newton's role as an MP allowed him to represent the interests of the academic community within the English government. This was particularly important during a time when universities and scientific institutions were seeking greater influence and funding from the state.
2. **Political Connections**: Serving in Parliament helped Newton build valuable connections with influential political figures. These connections were instrumental in securing his later appointments and in garnering support for his scientific and administrative initiatives.
3. **Administrative Reforms**: As Master of the Mint, Newton implemented numerous administrative reforms to improve efficiency and productivity. He modernized the Mint's operations, introducing new machinery and processes that increased the output of high-quality coins. Newton's management skills ensured that the Mint operated effectively, even during periods of high demand.

Other Political and Administrative Contributions

1. **Adviser and Consultant**: Newton's expertise in various fields made him a sought-after adviser and consultant. He provided advice on a range of issues, from economic policy to scientific matters, leveraging his reputation and knowledge to influence decision-making processes.
2. **Public Engagement and Communication**: Newton understood the importance of public engagement and communication in promoting scientific knowledge. He supported initiatives to increase public awareness of scientific discoveries and their implications, helping to bridge the gap between the scientific community and the general public.

Isaac Newton's political and administrative roles showcased his ability to apply his analytical mind to practical and governance-related challenges. His contributions to the reformation of the coinage system, his leadership of the Royal Society, and his service as a Member of Parliament demonstrated his commitment to public service and his influence on both scientific and political spheres.

Newton's legacy in these roles is characterized by his meticulous approach to problem-solving, his dedication to improving public institutions, and his efforts to promote scientific knowledge and innovation. His work laid the foundation for modern practices in currency production, scientific governance, and public engagement, underscoring his enduring impact on both science and society.

6

Personal Life and Character

Personal Life and Character

Isaac Newton, one of the most influential scientists in history, had a complex personal life and a distinctive character that shaped his interactions with family, colleagues, and society at large. This chapter delves into his relationships, personality traits, habits, and religious views, offering a comprehensive picture of the man behind the monumental scientific achievements.

Relationships with Family and Colleagues

Family: Isaac Newton's relationships with his family were complicated and often strained. Born on Christmas Day, 1642, in Woolsthorpe, Lincolnshire, Newton faced early adversity. His father died before he was born, and his mother, Hannah Ayscough, remarried when he was three, leaving young Isaac in the care of his maternal grandmother. This separation had a profound impact on Newton, instilling in him a sense of abandonment that persisted throughout his life.

Newton's early experiences of loss and separation likely influenced his later solitary nature and intense focus on his work. When his mother returned to Woolsthorpe after the death of her second husband, their relationship remained distant and formal. Despite this strained relationship, Newton took on family responsibilities later in life, particularly helping his nieces and nephews. He never married and had no children, dedicating his life to his work and studies.

Colleagues: Newton's relationships with his colleagues were often marked by tension and conflict, stemming from his intense personality and intellectual rigor. His most notable scientific disputes included:

1. **Robert Hooke:** Newton had a contentious relationship with Hooke, a key figure in the Royal Society. Their disagreements over the nature of light and color, and Hooke's challenge to Newton's work on gravity, led to a bitter rivalry that affected their professional interactions. Hooke criticized Newton's theories on optics, leading Newton to be defensive and protective of his work. The rivalry became so intense that, after Hooke's death, Newton allegedly ensured that no known portrait of Hooke remained in the Royal Society.
2. **Gottfried Wilhelm Leibniz:** Newton's dispute with Leibniz over the invention of calculus is one of the most famous scientific controversies. Both men developed calculus independently, but accusations of plagiarism and priority disputes created a deep rift between them and their respective supporters. This controversy polarized the mathematical community in Europe and had lasting impacts on the development of calculus and mathematical notation.
3. **John Flamsteed:** Newton's relationship with John Flamsteed, the Astronomer Royal, was strained due to disagreements over access to astronomical data and the publication of Flamsteed's star catalog without his consent. Newton's impatience and Flamsteed's protective stance over his data led to a significant conflict that soured their professional relationship.

Despite these conflicts, Newton also had positive relationships with some contemporaries. Notably, his relationship with Edmund Halley was fruitful and collaborative. Halley encouraged Newton to write the "Principia Mathematica" and even financed its publication. Halley's support and friendship were crucial to Newton's success in publishing one of the most important works in the history of science.

Personality Traits and Habits

Isaac Newton's personality was marked by several distinctive traits and habits that shaped his life and work:

1. **Intellectual Rigor:** Newton was known for his meticulous and methodical approach to scientific inquiry. His dedication to precision and detail was evident in his experiments and writings, setting high standards for scientific research. He often worked late into the night, driven by an insatiable curiosity and a relentless pursuit of understanding.
2. **Solitude:** Newton was a solitary figure, often preferring the company of books and experiments over social interactions. His reclusive nature allowed him to focus intensely on his work but also contributed to his sometimes difficult relationships with others. Newton would often retreat into long periods of isolation, during which he would make some of his most significant discoveries.
3. **Persistence and Determination:** Newton's persistence in solving complex problems was legendary. He spent years working on his theories of gravity, motion, and optics, often revisiting and refining his ideas until he was satisfied with their accuracy. His determination to solve problems, no matter how challenging, was a hallmark of his scientific career.

4. **Paranoia and Secrecy:** Newton was known to be paranoid about his work being stolen or plagiarized. This led him to be secretive about his discoveries, delaying the publication of many of his findings. He was particularly guarded about his alchemical research, much of which he kept private.
5. **Temperament:** Newton could be irritable and argumentative, especially when his ideas were challenged. His intense focus on his work sometimes made him impatient with those who did not meet his high intellectual standards. He was known to have fierce debates and was not easily swayed from his positions once he had formed an opinion.

Religious Views

Isaac Newton's religious beliefs were complex and deeply personal. He was a devout Christian, but his views often diverged from mainstream Anglican doctrine. Key aspects of his religious views include:

1. **Anti-Trinitarianism:** Newton rejected the doctrine of the Trinity, a fundamental tenet of mainstream Christianity. He believed in the unity of God and considered the Trinity to be a corrupt interpretation of Christianity. His anti-Trinitarian views were heretical by the standards of his time, and he kept them largely private to avoid persecution. Despite his unorthodox beliefs, Newton remained deeply religious and saw his scientific work as a means of understanding God's creation.
2. **Biblical Scholarship:** Newton devoted considerable time to the study of the Bible and theology. He believed that the Bible contained hidden truths and prophecies that could be unlocked through careful analysis. His theological writings, including "Observations upon the Prophecies of Daniel and

the Apocalypse of St. John," reflect his deep interest in scriptural interpretation. Newton meticulously studied the Bible, seeking to reconcile his scientific discoveries with his faith.

3. **Rational Faith:** Newton's approach to religion was rational and evidence-based. He sought to reconcile his scientific understanding of the natural world with his religious beliefs, viewing the universe as a creation of a rational and omnipotent God. Newton saw no conflict between science and religion; rather, he believed that studying the natural world was a way to glorify God.

4. **Alchemical Interests:** Newton's interest in alchemy was intertwined with his religious views. He believed that alchemical processes could reveal the divine principles governing the natural world and sought to uncover these secrets through his alchemical experiments. Alchemy, for Newton, was not just a quest for material transformation but also a spiritual pursuit.

> **Fun Fact: Apple Story:** The famous story of an apple falling on Newton's head is likely apocryphal, but it is based on a real event. Newton himself recounted that he was inspired to think about gravity while observing an apple fall from a tree, leading him to ponder why objects fall straight down rather than moving sideways or upward.

Isaac Newton's personal life and character were as complex and multifaceted as his scientific achievements. His relationships with family and colleagues were often strained, influenced by his intense personality and solitary nature. His intellectual rigor, persistence, and determination drove his groundbreaking work, while his paranoia and secrecy reflected his fear of intellectual theft.

Newton's religious views were unorthodox and deeply personal, shaping his approach to both science and theology. His belief in a rational, divinely ordered universe underpinned his scientific inquiries and his biblical scholarship.

Overall, Newton's personal life and character played a crucial role in shaping his legacy as one of the greatest scientists in history. His relentless pursuit of knowledge, combined with his complex personality and deep religious convictions, left an indelible mark on the fields of mathematics, physics, and beyond. Through his scientific discoveries, administrative roles, and philosophical reflections, Newton's influence continues to resonate in the modern world, inspiring countless generations of scientists and thinkers.

> **Fun Fact: Knighted by Queen Anne:** Newton was knighted by Queen Anne in 1705, primarily for his political services rather than his scientific achievements. He was the second scientist to be knighted, following Sir Francis Bacon.

7

Recognition and Honors

Isaac Newton's extraordinary contributions to science and mathematics earned him numerous awards, honors, and recognition during his lifetime. Even after his death, his legacy has been preserved and celebrated through various institutions and memorials. This chapter explores the recognition Newton received during his lifetime, as well as the posthumous honors that have ensured his lasting impact on science and society.

Awards, Honors, and Recognition During His Lifetime

1. **Fellowship at Trinity College:** In 1667, Newton was elected a fellow of Trinity College, Cambridge, following his remarkable academic performance and early research contributions. This fellowship provided him with the financial support and academic freedom to pursue his research in mathematics and natural philosophy.
2. **Lucasian Professorship:** In 1669, Newton succeeded his mentor, Isaac Barrow, as the Lucasian Professor of Mathematics at Cambridge University. This prestigious position allowed Newton to continue his research and teaching. The Lucasian Professorship is one of the most esteemed academic positions in the field of mathematics.

3. **Election to the Royal Society:** Newton was elected a Fellow of the Royal Society (FRS) in 1672, shortly after presenting his work on the reflecting telescope and his theories on light and color. The Royal Society, one of the world's oldest and most respected scientific institutions, recognized Newton's contributions and provided a platform for him to share his research with other leading scientists.
4. **Knighting by Queen Anne:** In 1705, Newton was knighted by Queen Anne during a visit to Cambridge. This honor was in recognition of his contributions to science and his service to the country, particularly his role in reforming the coinage system as Warden and later Master of the Mint. Newton's knighthood was a significant mark of royal favor and public recognition.
5. **Recognition for the Principia Mathematica:** The publication of "Philosophiæ Naturalis Principia Mathematica" (Mathematical Principles of Natural Philosophy) in 1687 brought Newton international acclaim. The "Principia" was widely recognized as a monumental work in the history of science, and it solidified Newton's reputation as one of the greatest scientists of his time. Scientists, mathematicians, and philosophers across Europe lauded the groundbreaking theories and mathematical rigor of the work.
6. **Professional and Social Influence:** Newton held several influential positions throughout his career, including President of the Royal Society from 1703 until his death in 1727. His leadership and influence extended beyond his scientific work, impacting the direction and priorities of the scientific community in Britain and beyond.

Posthumous Honors and Preservation of His Legacy

1. **Burial in Westminster Abbey:** Newton was buried in Westminster Abbey in London, an honor reserved for the most distinguished individuals in British history. His tomb in the Abbey is inscribed with a Latin epitaph praising his unparalleled contributions to science and mathematics.
2. **Memorials and Monuments:** Numerous statues, monuments, and memorials have been erected in Newton's honor. These include a statue in the chapel of Trinity College, Cambridge, and another in the courtyard of the British Library in London. These memorials celebrate Newton's legacy and inspire future generations of scientists and scholars.
3. **Newton's Image on Currency:** Newton's image has appeared on various forms of currency, including British banknotes and coins. His depiction on the £1 note from 1978 to 1988 highlighted his lasting impact on British culture and his contributions to the nation's scientific heritage.

Isaac Newton Institute

RECOGNITION AND HONORS

4. **Institutions Named After Newton:** Numerous scientific institutions, schools, and awards bear Newton's name. For example, the Isaac Newton Institute for Mathematical Sciences in Cambridge is a leading center for research in mathematics. The Newton Medal, awarded by the Institute of Physics, recognizes outstanding contributions to physics.

> **Fun Fact: Newton's Hair Sample:** A sample of Newton's hair, preserved after his death, was analyzed in the 20th century. The analysis revealed high levels of mercury, likely from his alchemical experiments, suggesting possible exposure to toxic substances during his research.

5. **The Newtonian Legacy in Education:** Newton's works, particularly the "Principia Mathematica" and "Opticks," continue to be studied in physics and mathematics curricula worldwide. His theories form the foundation of classical mechanics, and his methodological approach to scientific inquiry remains a model for researchers.

6. **Commemoration in Astronomy:** Newton's contributions to astronomy and physics are commemorated by the naming of celestial bodies and features in his honor. For example, there is a crater on the Moon named "Newton" and an asteroid designated as "8000 Isaac Newton."

> **Fun Fact: Newton's Apple Tree:** The famous story of Newton's inspiration for the theory of gravity supposedly came from an apple falling from a tree. The tree, believed to be the original or a descendant of it, still stands at Woolsthorpe Manor, Newton's birthplace, and attracts many visitors.

7. **Influence on Popular Culture:** Newton's life and work have been depicted in numerous books, films, and other media. His story continues to captivate the public imagination, reflecting his enduring legacy as one of history's greatest scientists.

Isaac Newton's lifetime achievements garnered significant recognition and honors, reflecting his monumental contributions to science and mathematics. His posthumous legacy is preserved through numerous memorials, institutions, and cultural references. Newton's work continues to influence contemporary science and mathematics, ensuring his place as a towering figure in the history of human knowledge.